DIE ZAHLENGESCHICHTE

THE NUMBER STORY

SMALL BOOK ONE

ENGLISH - GERMAN

*Numbers Teach Children
Their Number Names*

written and illustrated by

MISS ANNA

Early Reader Edition of *The Number Story 1*
Bronze Medal Winner, 2016 Wishing Shelf Book Award

Library of Congress Control Number: 2018902040

Names: Miss Anna, author.
Title: Number story : numbers teach children their number names / Miss Anna.
Description: Portland, OR: Lumpy Publishing, 2018.
Identifiers: ISBN 978-1-945977-18-3| LCCN 2018902040
Summary: The pictures and rhymes present stories which introduce numbers 0-10.
Subjects: LCSH Numeration—English--German--Pictorial works--Juvenile literature. | BISAC JUVENILE NONFICTION /
Languages: English--German
Classification: LCC QA141.3 .M57 2018 | DDC 513—dc23

Publisher: Lumpy Publishing
Website: www.missannabooks.com
Email: missanna@missannabooks.com

Paperback: ISBN 978-1-945977-18-3
Printed in the U.S.A.   1 3 5 7 9 10 8 6 4 2

Möchtest du die Namen
der Zahlen lernen?

It is very easy and a lot of fun!

Es ist sehr einfach und macht viel Spaß!

Say-along our little jingle

Singe mit uns unsere kleine Geschichte!

starting from Number One!

Wir beginnen mit der Zahl Eins!

1

ONE looks like my one finger.

EINS

sieht aus wie mein Finger.

ONE!
EINS!

2

TWO   trails a tail.

ZWEI

zeichnet einen Tierschwanz.

A TAIL!

EINEN TIERSCHWANZ!

3

THREE   has bumps.

DREI

hat Höcker.

BUMPY! HÖCKERIG!

4

FOUR carries a sail.

VIER

trägt ein Segel.

A SAIL!
EIN SEGEL!

5

FIVE   is a racing track.

FÜNF

ist eine Rennstrecke.

VROOM
BRUMM!
1

SIX curves like a snail.

SECHS

Kurvt sich wie eine Schnecke.

A SNAIL! EINE SCHNECKE!

7

SEVEN has a sharp angle.

SIEBEN

hat eine scharfe Kante.

OUCH!
AUA!

8

EIGHT   is rollercoaster rails.

ACHT

ist eine Achterbahnschiene.

HURRA!
YIPPEE!

NINE   is a bubble on a stick.

NEUN

ist eine Blase auf einem Stock.

A BUBBLE! EINE BLASE!

10

TEN is an eye of a whale.

ZEHN

ist das Auge eines Wals.

WINK!
ZWINKERN!

And
Und

0

ZERO   is an empty pail.

NULL

ist ein leerer Eimer.

IT'S EMPTY!
Er ist leer!

Thank you for playing with us today.

We had a lot of fun too!

Danke, dass du heute mit uns gespielt hast. Wir hatten auch so viel Spaß!

We are your Number friends,
Zero to Ten,
Who will be here for you~
Wir sind deine Zahlenfreunde,
Null bis Zehn.
Wir werden immer für dich da sein!

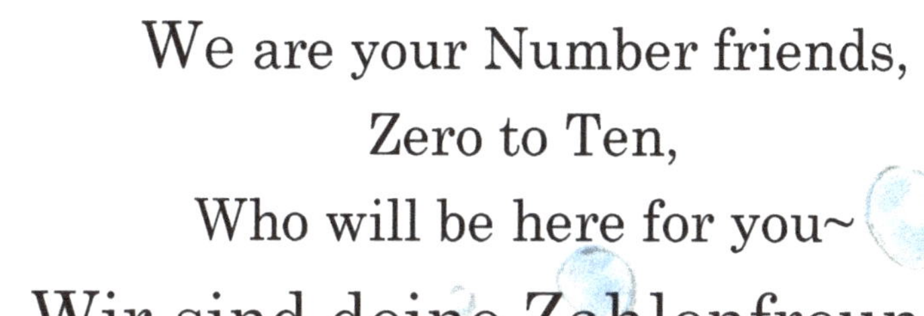

Bye-bye now!
See you again soon!
Tschüss erstmal!
Wir sehen uns bald wieder!

The Numbers are *SINGING* too!

To sing-a-long, look for Miss Anna Number Story
at your favorite music store like iTUNES.

MP3

Numbers 0-10
IDENTIFYING
& COUNTING

Numbers 11-20
& Ordinals
first, second, third...

Numbers 0-100
& Place Values
ones, tens, hundreds...

About Clocks
& Telling Time
hours, minutes, seconds...

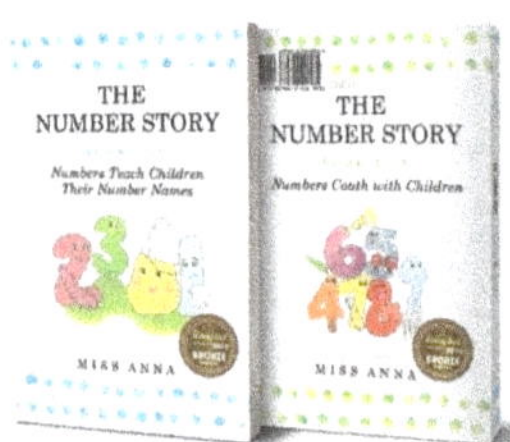

Number Story 1 & 2
isbn: 978-0-996216-48-7

Number Story 3 & 4
isbn: 978-1-945977-01-5

Number Story 5 & 6
isbn: 978-1-945977-06-0

Number Story 7 & 8
isbn: 978-1-949320-40-

For more Miss Anna books to love,
visit us at

www.missannabooks.com

Numbers are working hard all over the world!
Come Travel the World with Us!